FRANZ
KAFKA
and Prague

Karol Kállay

Franz K

afka and Prague

Karol Kállay

Franz Kafka and Prague
© 1996, 2001 by Slovart Publishing Ltd.

Idea, selections of quotations and photographies: *Karol Kállay*
Foreword: *Eduard Goldstücker*
Research of quotations in English translations: *Alice Sniegonová*
Updating of older translations and translation of untranslated quotations: *Josef Čermák*
Graphic Design: *Branislav Gajdoš*
Editor: *Jana Steinerová*
Art Editor: *Ladislav Donauer*
Print: Neografia, a. s., Martin

ISBN 80-7145-575-X

I write differently to how I speak, and I speak differently to how I think, and so it continues, right to the deepest darkness.

Letters to Ottla and Family

Franz Kafka was born and lies buried in Prague. It was his home for virtually his whole lifetime; only a few months before his death did he, after years of hesitation, make up his mind to leave it. The following pages intend to outline briefly the specific character of Prague as the background and environment of that life.

At Kafka's birth a provincial city of less than 300,000 inhabitants. Prague more than doubled its population during his lifetime and became the capital of the newly created Czechoslovak Republic. But even the pre-1918 Prague was much more than simply a provincial city. It was the capital of the Kingdom of Bohemia, one of the historical constituents of Austria-Hungary, and the metropolis of that empire's economically most developed nation, whose national emancipation had just attained its highest phase.

It can be said without exaggeration that the most important single factor, which, in Kafka's time, affected the life of every Prague citizen was his place in the complicated, precarious coexistence of the city's three ethnic-religious components: the Czechs, the Germans and the Jews. For nobody, as long as he stayed in Prague – and often even at a distance –, could remain aloof from that entanglement.

When Kafka was born, Prague looked back at more than thousand years of recorded history in which, from very early on, it had been a domicile of those three communities. It emerged from the mythical haze around its matriarchal foundress, Princess Libuše, as the main settlement of the tribe that gave its name to the westernmost branch of the Slavs and, in the course of time, became the capital of the Czech state. As such, it soon contained a considerable German colony upon which Prince Soběslav, at the end of the eleventh century, conferred a special statute, while the presence in Prague of a Jewish community is documented since the tenth century.

Living in such an ancient city, Kafka's contemporaries could not avoid the awareness of its turbulent past; mementos stood plenti-ful along their daily paths. – During the greater part of the 14th century, as the capital of the Holy Roman Empire, Prague ranked among Europe's foremost cities, to become, soon after, the center of the Hussite movement causing, among other things, the exodus first of the German scholars of the University, then of almost all German burghers. The Hussite revolution, the first serious challenge of the authority of the Pope and the

Emperor, inaugurated an era of religious unrest which left its deep imprint on Prague's destinies.

The religiously motivated tug-of-war went on for generations. When, at long last, under Rudolph II. (when Prague again was the Empire's capital), the warring parties concluded a truce, it proved to be short-lived because, precarious as it was in itself, it could not withstand the growing political tensions of contemporaty Europe. Its breach provoked the Protestant Bohemian Estates to rebel, in 1618, against the Habsburg dynasty and thereby, unwittingly, to fire the first shots of the Thirty Years War. When the rebellion was defeated, two years later, in the fateful Battle of the White Mountain outside Prague, the city and the whole country with its up to 80 per cent non-Catholic inhabitants, found themselves at the twofold mercy of the Emperor's sword and the Pope's crusade. As a result, Bohemia was deprived of its independence for three hundred years; all freemen unwilling to convert to Catholicism were dispossessed and forced into exile, whereby the Czechs lost their upper social classes and, consisting only of peasant masses and lowest urban strata, were for the next two centuries reduced virtually to the existence of "a nation without history". Public administration as well as the towns were soon Germanized, the majority of the population was forcibly reverted to Catholicism under a relentless pressure that finally subsided only with the Patent of Toleration of 1781.

But by then the first clouds of a new storm had begun to loom just beyond the horizon; they were those of the Czech-German national conflict which, from then on, gathered force, broke into the open in 1848, and until 1918 (in a wider dimension really until the late 1940's) dominated human affairs to such an extent that it earned Bohemia the attribute of "the classic land of national strife".

To complete the sketch of Prague as the background to Kafka's life, it is necessary to add that the Habsburg Empire came into being primarily as a bulwark against the Turkish menace. Once the Turks had been pushed back, that conglomeration of kingdoms, duchies, principalities etc. under the Habsburg rule lost its original "raison d'être", and had subsequently proved incapable of finding a new one – one which could have given it a degree of cohesion and viability sufficient to overcome the Empire's backwardness and to weather out the storms of nationalism. The measures taken in this respect by successive governments since the middle of the 18th century generally legged a step or two behind the times. Because of this ingrained "too little and too late", Austria-Hungary was, by the turn of our century, the only great power with a question-mark hanging not merely over its internal regime but over its very existence.

The situation of the Prague Germans reflected in a peculiar way that of the

Monarchy as a whole in that they, too, had a considerable past but a problematical future. They were an ethnic enclave encompassed by Czechs, socially mainly upper class without a popular basis, a minority decreasing, during Kafka's life, from about 40,000 to around 30,000 and it relative terms from approximately 15 to 7 per cent of the city's population. Yes it was the German patriciate thad had administered Prague for two and a half centuries until the 1860's when a change in the property clauses of the electoral law led to the emergence of a Czech majority.

In the light of recent experience one can identify the frame of mind present among the Prague Germans as similar to that which was – and still is – typical for colonial settlers in the course of de-colonisation, and recognise the Czech-German contest in the inner regions of the Czech lands (including Prague) as a process of de-colonisation as it were *avant la lettre*. Because of the long past preponderance of the German element, German nationalists regarded Prague as a German city, and sought to reinforce their claim by citing two additional factors specific to Prague:

1. The Prague Germans had at their disposal a cultural establishment (comprising, among others, two universities, two theatres, two – in Kafka's last years even three – notable daily papers) which was out of proportion, in its variety and importance, to their actual size.

2. Prague housed two kinds of Germans: permanent residents, and a fluctuating complement consisting mainly of students from the country's border districts (the later so-called Sudetenland). The latter were the principal and vociferous champions of German nationalistic militancy fed, in the period under discussion increasingly, from sources in the neighbouring German Reich. The idea of a Germanic retreat anywhere in the world grew more repugnant – and this is one of the important facets of Habsburg Austria's tragedy – the more the strength and the aspirations of the Wilhelmine Empire intensified.

As á result of all this, the German residents of Prague felt their city as inscrutably strange in its exquisite beauty, as if streching beyond the confines of rationally explicable reality, as if containing vague threats behind its facades. Their literary productions of that time frequently testify to their authors' fascination with, and mystification by, the past. In retrospect, all this can be seen as symptomatic of the psychological attitude of people living in a small beleaguered island. It seems as if their Janus-like city was turned towards them with its aged, backward-looking face, signalling the imminent end of a great epoch.

For the Czechs, by contrast, Prague was the centre of their national life, endearingly referred to as Prague the "little mother", a monument to past glory and a promise of its future renewal. The Czech Prague had a steady influx of people from the provinces attracted by its growing industry, trade, and expanding cultural life, and saw the Czech middle classes, practically non-existent a few decades earlier, growing in numbers and in economic as well as political significance.

The situation of the Jews in Prague bore a somewhat special character owing not only to the fact that they were one of the oldest. Jewish communities in those parts of Europe, but that for a century and a half, up to the beginning of the 19th century, Prague was the largest Jewish settlement in the world.

From the very beginning of the Czech-German confrontation, the Jews were cought up between the two warring camps. The law of the land had kept them for centuries apart from the rest of the population as an alien body, strictly controlled and tolerated in assigned places of residence solely by the ruler's permission which was revokable at any moment. The first opportunity of a partial integration into a non-Jewish society was opened to them at the end of the 18th century by a policy designed to modernize the Empire. It was an integration on the basis of the German language. When the Czech national re-awakening got into its stride, it found the Jews of Prague already belonging, linguistically and culturally, to the German element of the city, and confronted them with virulent antisemitism. A distinction must be made here between the Czech a German attitude towards the Jews. The difference stemmed from the fact that the Czechs, much more than the Germans, felt the Jews to be economic competitors. One of the principal problems of the Czech national revival was to recreate an indigenous middle class and thus replace its loss some two hundred years previously. The Jews, as it happened, were occupying those lower positions in trade the Czechs aimed at as their first objectives. The Germans, naturally interested in keeping the Jews within their camp, were constantly warning them against any rapprochement with the Czechs by depicting these as primitive, barbaric antisemites. Thus, for some decades, the Germans maintained – at least outwardly – a sort of enlightened liberal attitude towards the Jews, while Czech nationalism made ample use of antisemitic agitation. But from about the time of Kafka's birth, this situation began to change substantially with the emergence, and political impact, of "modern" antisemitism founded no longer on age-old religious resentment but on racialism. And even though the Germans of Prague remained on the whole immune to it, it made itself felt through shock waves from Vienna and Berlin, and directly from the Sudetenland, especially at the Prague German Universities.

Although this racialist antisemitism soon grew into an international movement, to the Prague Jews it came first as a German invention and confronted the with new problems. In consequence, their trust in the "civilized" Germans as against the "primitive" Czechs markedly diminished and the very notion of assimilation became questionable again. Kafka's dispariging remarks about *Wustjudentum* are related to this problem. They stem from the feeling of finding oneself in a blind alley or on swampland without solid ground under one's feet for having followed the light of assimilation which turned out to be but a mirage. Western (and since then not only Western) societies have, with the one hand, been offering the Jews integration through assimilation, while, with the other hand, erecting obstacles to prevent it.

As a result, there appeared various attempts at a readjustment to the new situation. Generally, the Prague Jews tried, in this last phase of the Habsburg rule, to keep clear of the cross-fire by maintaining a neutral position in the Czech-German struggle. A considerable number hoped to find refuge in the Czech camp which, meanwhile, had increased its strength in many respects (in the census of 1890, 74 per cents of Prague Jews registered German as their language while in 1900 only 45 per cent did so). The idea of Jewish nationalism, when it eventually appeared, found a fertile soil in Prague. Some sought a solution in leaving Prague altogether. All these are symptoms of an impaired sense of security and of man intensified quest for identity.

Eduard Goldstücker

I see a town in the distance. Is that the one you meant? It's possible. However I don't understand how you can make out a town where, even when you point it out, I see only a few faint outlines in the mist.

Oh yes, I see it, the mountain up there with a castle, and on the slopes a settlement that resembles a village.

So it is the town – in a way a large village – you're right.

Fragments from Notebooks and Loose Sheets

It is a town between towns, whose past is greater than its present, but even that is still quite remarkable.

Fragments from Notebooks and Loose Sheets

We were living in the house which separates the Little Square from the Old Town Square.

Letters to Milena

Does one suspect, perhaps, that I was educated in some out-of-way place? No, I was educated in the middle of the city, in the middle of the city.

The Diaries

...there are dark lanes there, godforsaken houses with passage-ways, even a small square immersed in twilight and cold...

Fragments from Notebooks and Loose Sheets

Our cook, a small dry thin person with a pointed nose, hollow cheeks, somewhat jaundiced but firm, energetic, and superior took me to school every morning.

Letters to Milena

...the Jacob Church was striking 8, you could hear the school's bells, other children would start to run – I always had the greatest terror of being late – now we had to run as well...

Letters to Milena

Then I looked out of my chair through the open window into the rain…

Letters to Milena

It is not necessary that you leave the house. Remain at your table and listen. Do not even listen, only wait. Do not even wait, be wholly still and alone. The world will present itself to you for its unmasking, it can do no other, in ecstasy it will writhe at your feet.

The Collected Aphorisms

Are you trying to make me believe I'm unreal, standing here on the green pavement?

Description of a Struggle

If people must build such huge squares from sheer wantonness, why don't they build a balustrade across them as well?

Description of a Struggle

You, sky… and as for you, Old Town Square, you never have been real.

Description of a Struggle

The suburbs of our native city, however, are also foreign to us, but in this case comparisons have value, a half-hour's walk can prove it to us over and over again, here live people partly within our city, partly on the miserable, dark edge of the city that is furrowed like a great ditch, although they all have as great an area of common interests as no other group of people outside the city. For this reason I always enter and leave the suburb with a weak mixed feeling of anxiety, of abandonment, of sympathy, of curiosity, of conceit, of joy in travelling, of fortitude, and return with pleasure, seriousness, and calm, especially from Žižkov.

The Diaries

Today, for that matter, is the first day I perceived the town. Among these people nothing good can happen, but a lot of good things happen to them.

Letters to Ottla and Family

I recall the first night. At the time we lived in Celetná Street...

Letters to Milena

But as I passed through the front door with short steps I was assaulted from the sky by moon and stars and a great vaulted expanse, and from the Old Town Square by the Town Hall, the Virgin's pillar, the church.

Description of a Struggle

And now the torture of running back to the Old Town Square!

Letters to Milena

So you first had to cross the Old Town Square, then turn onto the Týnská Lane, then proceed through a kind of vaulted gate on to the Meat Market Street and down to the Meat Market.

Letters to Milena

In us all it still lives - the dark corners, the secret alleys, shuttered windows, squalid courtyards, rowdy pubs, and sinister inns. We walk through the broad streets of the newly built town. But our steps and our glances are uncertain. Inside we tremble just as before in the ancient streets of our misery. Our heart knows nothing of the slum clearance which has been achieved. The unhealthy Jewish town within us is far more real than the new hygienic town around us. Awake we walk in a dream — alone like mere phantoms of bygone days.

Gustav Janouch: Conversations with Kafka

Yesterday evening, at ten o' clock, I was walking at my sad pace down the Celetná Street. Near the Hess hat store a young man stops three steps in front of me, so forces me to stop too, removes his hat, and then runs at me.

The Diaries

Which land is it in? I can't tell. Everything corresponds with everything there, and everything fuses gradually into everything else. I know that land is somewhere . . . I even see it. It's just that I don't know where it is, and I cannot get near it.

Fragments from Notebooks and Loose Sheets

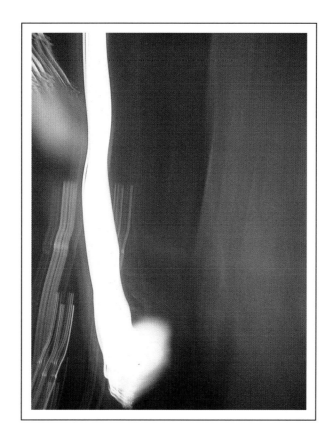

Every person carries within them some room. You can verify this by listening. If we listen to the rapid pacing of someone, say at night, when everything about is quiet: we can hear the rattle of a loosely hung mirror against the wall.

First Octavo Notebook

What now? Go check the house in the Ovocná Street. It's quiet, no one going in, no one going out, I wait a little, first in front of the house and then across the street: nothing – houses like that are so much wiser than the people who stare at them.

Letters to Milena

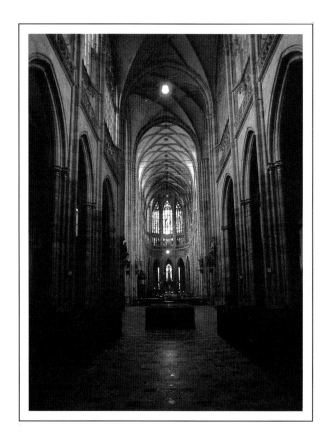

In the distance a large triangle of candle flames flickered on the high altar. K. could not have said with certainty whether he had seen them earlier on.

The Trial

The square in front of the cathedral was deserted ... The cathedral too seemed empty, of course nobody would think of coming here now.

The Trial

But was a sermon really going to be delivered? Could K. by himself be regarded as a congregation? What if he were a stranger who had come there only to look at the church? And of course that is what he was. It was senseless to think a sermon was to be preached now, at eleven o' clock on a weekday in the most horrible weather.

The Trial

$\mathcal{K}$. returned to the main entrance, stood there irresolutely
for a while, then walked round the outside of the cathedral in the
rain in case the Italian might perhaps be waiting at
a side-entrance.

The Trial

A. is a virtuoso and heaven is his witness.

The Collected Aphorisms

October 18, 1917. Fear in the night. Fear of that which is beyond the night.

Third Octavo Notebook

At the time we lived in the Celetná Street... It was summer, very hot, probably this time of year, completely unbearable. I kept stopping in front of the window...

Letters to Milena

A town resembles the sun: in the centre of the circle all light is concentrated, dazzling. A person can wander lost through the streets, the houses. Once he has entered it, then, somehow, he can never get out...

Fragments from Notebooks and Loose Sheets

It is my old native town, and slowly, hesitantly I wander through its streets.

Fragments from Notebooks and Loose Sheets

Save that my thoughts grew blurred at this moment, for the
Vltava and the quarter of the town on the farther shore lay together
in the dark. A number of lights burning there teased the eye.

Description of a Struggle

*And as we walked home over the Charles Bridge toward
morning – it was still hot and beautiful – I was actually happy . . .*

Letters to Milena

This is a place where I never was before: one's breath comes differently, more dazzling than the sun is the radiance of a star beside it.

The Collected Aphorisms

...empty streets, clean and quiet; somewhere a window which was swinging free is slowly closed; somewhere the corners of a scarf, thrown over a balcony railing high above the street, flutter; somewhere an open window with a curtain moving lightly in the wind, otherwise no movement... anywhere.

Fragments from Notebooks and Loose Sheets

...then still larger rings, and the light already so dispersed that a person must search them out, those large tracts of the city which still lie in a cold grey light.

Fragments from Notebooks and Loose Sheets

Dreams rolled over me. I lay tired and hopeless on the bed.

Fifth Octavo Notebook

There is a goal, but no way, what we call a way is hesitation.

The Collected Aphorisms

Nothing came of it . . . just residues of light traversing the words.

Fragments from Notebooks and Loose Sheets

What have I in common with Jews? I have hardly anything in common with myself and should stand very quietly in a corner, content that I can breathe.

The Diaries

But when I reached the cemetery I couldn't find the grave, the information booth was closed, no attendant and none of the women knew a thing. I also checked in a book but it was the wrong one, I wandered around for hours, completely befuddled from reading the inscriptions and left the cemetery in a similar state...

Letters to Milena

One more small decoration for this grave. Is it not decorated enough already? Yes, but in view of the fact that I'm such an old hand at it...

Fragments from Notebooks and Loose Sheets

...sometimes you amazed me by being able to show me in the prayer book the passage that was being said at the moment, and for the rest, so long as I was present in the synagogue (and this was the main thing) I was allowed to hang around wherever I liked.

Letter to his Father

I was stirred immeasurably more deeply by Judaism in the Pinkas Synagogue.

The Diaries

But what sort of Judaism was it that I got from you?
In the course of the years, I have taken roughly three attitudes
to it.

As a child I reproached myself, in accord with you, for not
going to the synagogue often enough, for not fasting, and so on.
I thought that in this way I was doing a wrong not to myself
but to you, and I was penetrated by a sense of guilt, which was,
of course, always near at hand.

Letter to his Father

I have written nothing for so long because of having arranged an evening for Löwy in the banquet room of the Jewish Town Hall on 18 February 1912, at which I delivered a little introductory lecture on Yiddish.

The Diaries

The house was already locked. There was light in two of the windows on the second floor and in one window on the fourth floor. A car pulled up in front of the house. A young man came to the lighted window on the fourth floor and opened it, looking down on the street. In the light of the moon.

The Diaries

Perhaps I'm not allowed to remain too long in one place; there are people who can acquire a sense of home only when they are travelling.

Letters to Friends, Family and Editors

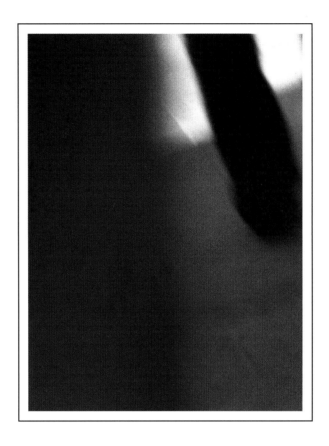

The true way leads along a tight-rope, which is not stretched aloft but just above the ground. It seems designed more to trip one than to be walked along.

The Collected Aphorisms

You came too late. He was here. In the autumn he doesn't stay long in the same spot. He's drawn outside to the dark boundless fields, just as the crows are. If you want to see him run out to the fields, he will definitely be there.

Fragments from Notebooks and Loose Sheets

I have been here in the city for more than twenty years already. Can you even imagine what that means? I have spent each season here twenty times... The trees have been growing here for twenty years, how small should a person become under them. And all these nights, you know, in all the houses. Now you lie against this, now against that wall, so that the window keeps moving around you.

The Diaries

It's only that I'm so exhausted from all the walks, today up on the Vyšehrad Escarpment.

Letters to Milena

After you left there was a large windstorm at Jelení příkop, perhaps coincidence, perhaps not. Yesterday I overslept in the palace; when I came up to the small house, the fire was already out and long cold.

Letters to Ottla and Family

...it will always be finer to go across the bridge to the Belvedere than to go through the river into heaven.

Letters to Friends, Family and Editors

All right then, if you insist, I'll go with you, but I repeat: it's ridiculous to climb up the Petřin now, in winter and in the middle of the night.

Description of a Struggle

Down on the river lay several boats, fishermen had cast their lines, it was a dreary day. Some youths, their legs crossed, were leaning against the railing of the dock.

The Diaries

People who dark bridges cross
passing saints
with feeble candles.
Clouds that parade across grey skies
passing churches
with darkening towers.
One who leans on the squared stone rilling,
looking into the evening waters
hands resting upon ancient stone.

Letter to Oskar Pollak, 1903

Sorry. Upstairs. That long corridor. I opened a door and it wasn't mine. "Sorry," I said and turned to leave. But I discerned the man who lived there, slim and beardless with pursed lips, sitting at a small table with just an oil lamp on it.

First Octavo Notebook

I asked a traveller I met on the road if beyond the seven seas lie the seven deserts and beyond them the seven mountains, on the seventh mountain a castle and...

Fragments from Notebooks and Loose Sheets

Long, long ago I wanted to visit that town. It's a large lively place with many thousands of people living there. No stranger is ever turned away.

Fragments from Notebooks and Loose Sheets

In that town it is forever early morning, as if even the morning had hardly begun. A uniform sky, barely clarifying the grey...

Fragments from Notebooks and Loose Sheets

Fog in the town. Down the narrow lane, with one wall overgrown with ivy.

Fragments from Notebooks and Loose Sheets

Yesterday evening on the Belvedere and under the stars.

The Diaries

*Run. Run. The view from the next lane. Tall houses,
a still taller church.*

Fragments from Notebooks and Loose Sheets

And it really was kind of the moon to shine on me, too, and out of modesty I was about to place myself under the arch of the Old Town Bridge Tower when it occurred to me that the moon, of course, shone on everything.

Description of a Struggle

Last week I really belonged in this street I live on, which I call "Suicide Lane"…

Letters to Friends, Family and Editors

There's a door in my apartment which I never noticed until now. It's in the wall in the bedroom, which adjoins the neighbouring house. I never gave it a thought, let alone knew it was there.

Fragments from Notebooks and Loose Sheets

Nothing, except for an image, nothing else, utter oblivion.

Fragments from Notebooks and Loose Sheets

*I have nothing to lose and everything to gain if I give
in my notice and leave Prague. I risk nothing since my life in
Prague leads to nothing good.*

Letters to Ottla and Family

To want death but not pain is a bad sign. Otherwise one can risk death. One has simply been sent out as a biblical dove, and having found nothing green, now slips back into the darkness of the ark.

Letters to Milena

He has evidently seen the time on the clock of the Old Town Water Tower.

Description of a Struggle

Prague doesn't let go. Either of us. This old crone has claws. One has to yield, or else. We would have to set fire to it on two sides, at the Vyšehrad and at the Hradčany, then it would be possible for us to get away.

Letters to Friends, Family and Editors

I didn't portray people, I didn't tell stories, they're just images, only images.

Janouch's report of Kafka's comment on his prose-piece "The Stoker"

Beyond a certain point there is no return. This point has to be reached.

The Collected Aphorisms

Photos